☑ T5-CCK-530

CLIMBING THE RAINBOW

Teaching Spiritual Object Lessons

Coleman Graphics
99 Milbar Blvd.
Farmingdale, N.Y. 11735

Cover design by Coleman Graphics
Interior art by Sandra Pezoldt

Other books by Peggy Davison Jenkins, Ph.D.

ART FOR THE FUN OF IT:
A GUIDE FOR TEACHING YOUNG CHILDREN
(Prentice-Hall 1980)

THE MAGIC OF PUPPETRY:
A GUIDE FOR THOSE WORKING WITH YOUNG CHILDREN
(Prentice-Hall 1980)

Originally published and printed in
the United States of America by
The Association of Unity Churches
Youth Services
Unity Village, MO 64065

Second printing March, 1983
Manufactured in the United States of America
Coleman Graphics
99 Milbar Blvd.
Farmingdale, N.Y. 11735

ISBN 0-942494-48-2

ACKNOWLEDGMENTS

First I must acknowledge the powerful guidance of the set of books called A COURSE IN MIRACLES.

Next, I owe a debt of gratitude to the metaphysical ministers, teachers, and authors who have provided the inspiration for so many of the lessons in this book. During my years as a student of metaphysics, ideas and sources have blended into a whole, making it difficult for me to give isolated credit. Nevertheless, my gratitude goes to everyone who contributed to this work.

My very special thanks to Char Webster for her invaluable suggestions and editing help.

Appreciation goes to the artist, Sandra Pezoldt, for the many hours she lovingly contributed to this project.

Maggie Finefrock has my gratitude for her vision and backing, which spurred the book to completion.

DEDICATION

To the children of the world, that they may save time
on our journey homeward.

TABLE OF CONTENTS

LAYING THE FOUNDATION

A goal of this book is to help young people start believing the things that are true about themselves and to stop believing the things that are not true. When they know the truth about themselves, fantastic things begin to happen to them and to their world. They will provide the leadership needed to bring in the New Age.

Someone once said, "Woe to the man who has to learn principles in the time of crisis." The principles that children will learn in this book will help prepare them for whatever they may encounter in life. This is because they will come to understand that this is a mental and spiritual world, and whatever is in their lives is but the material expression of a belief in their minds. The backward thinking that sees the outside world as cause and themselves as effect will be corrected. They will come, hopefully, to see themselves as cause and the world as effect. The sound self-esteem that will result from working with these principles will help youngsters in whatever situations they may find themselves.

We are all given the choice of living in a physical world governed by material laws or in a world of mind governed by mental and spiritual laws. For every physical law, there is a parallel law in mind and spirit. Why not teach children to work with the higher laws as well as the physical? This will bring with it the gifts of peace, security, and confidence that will enable them to weather the storms of life.

The lessons that follow are simply to start the process. They are intended as aids for busy parents who are willing to take five minutes a day and teach some higher principles to their children. Many teachers, ministers, and counselors will find them usable, too. By no means does this group of lessons represent all the principles that need to be taught. They are simply those which meet the criteria of being quick to teach with household objects at the level of understanding of most elementary to high school age children.

The emphasis is on kitchen objects, as the lessons in the home would most likely take place there. Objects have long been a successful way of using the familiar to make clear the unfamiliar.

The highest kinds of learning are in symbols, not words, and easy-to-understand objects can symbolize many hard-to-understand truths.

Kahlil Gibran tells us, "Faith perceives Truth sooner than experience can." Your children may be short on experience but long on faith. You, as an adult, do not need to know all the answers to use these lessons. Just set the stage and tickle the children with these concepts which their own Inner Teacher can mold into perfect understanding.

Throughout the lesson it is of utmost importance to build the child's self-esteem. Never is the goal of the lesson more important than the feelings of the child. Always help him to feel good about himself.

You certainly do not have to be in full agreement with what is offered here; but if the ideas trigger your thinking and give you other ideas for teaching truths that are meaningful to you, the book will have served its purpose.

HOW TO USE THIS BOOK

Each lesson is intended to last approximately five minutes. For parents, five minutes onto the morning schedule is suggested as it is highly desirable to begin the child's day with this kind of food for thought. The mind, as well as the body, needs to be nourished. Or a parent may wish to use the lessons at bedtime or after school. The important thing is to have a regular schedule and to be consistent.

As there is no necessary sequence to the lessons, you may treat the book as a smorgasbord and pick and choose lessons depending on the needs of your children and your own interests. Watch for the "teachable moments."

The lessons are not written to be read to the child. They are for the adult to read and adapt to the child's level of understanding, augmented with personal examples.

It is better to cut the lessons short, leaving the child wanting a little more, than to exhaust the subject and bore the child. Studies with young children show that there is greater retention when a task is left incomplete. Rather than milk the analogy dry, just plan to revisit the idea occasionally.

The best formula for utilizing any of these lessons is "KISS" (Keep It Short and Simple). It will make a more lasting impression. The child's mind really doesn't need a lot of words and explanations. It is the adult mind that demands this.

The recommended procedure is to have the objects for the lesson already sitting on the table when the child arrives. This will intrigue him and build interest, maybe even suspense. Add to the drama a bit by having a special tray or mat on which the objects are placed. A most effective way to enhance the drama is to use a puppet or two to help teach the lesson.

There are lessons here for different levels of awareness. Make it okay to skip over any that do not appeal to you. If a lesson is not entirely accurate according to your philosophy, feel free to alter it or eliminate it. It is much better to teach the lessons you are excited about. This kind of enthusiasm is contagious. With children, often, much more is "caught than taught."

These lessons are designed to be adaptable to any age group from elementary to high school. Even if young people of diverse age groups are hearing a lesson together, they will each "get it" at their level of understanding. That is why specific scripts or explanations at the child's level are left out. You are then free to offer explanations that correspond to your level of metaphysical understanding.

It is urged that you read the lesson at least two days ahead of time, for a couple of reasons. One is so that you can be sure to have on hand whatever is needed. Most items are common to every household, but now and then there are a few exceptions. The other reason is that by reading the lessons ahead, you give your subconscious mind valuable time with the idea. You'll have a deeper understanding of it by the time of the lesson and, perhaps, a more meaningful way to present the idea. You can invite the creative subconscious mind to provide you with specific examples that your child will relate to. Please keep in mind that this material is intended to be open-ended so that you can take off with it in a way that is most in keeping with your belief system, while best meeting the needs of the children.

You may wish to end the lesson with an affirmation for each child or with a group affirmation. Affirmations are positive declarations of Truth and, as such, are powerful tools for changing one's thinking and attitudes, hence, one's experience. They are more fully explained in the chapter "Guidelines for Affirmations." In this case, the affirmation should be an outgrowth of each lesson. It can directly reinforce the lesson or relate to some concern of the child's which was revealed in the discussion of the lesson. Repeated use of the affirmation throughout the day can bring the child closer to the real truth about himself or herself.

Another suggestion is to be sure to allow time for input and questions from the children. Try not to make the lesson a straight monologue. Often children are closer to the "Truth" than we are and can teach us with their keen insights. Be willing to reverse roles and be the learner. It has been well said that "we teach what we are and what others are to us."

There may be times when it is impossible or totally inappropriate to use the objects involved in a lesson, but you still desire to get the message across. The next best thing to using objects is to paint a word picture. A picture in the mind can make a much more lasting impression than words without a visual image. For instance, a child can easily visualize a wastebasket of debris and a gift package hidden inside it (Lesson 20). A visual picture like that will more readily come to mind when needed than just eloquent words, such as, "There is the seed of advantage within every disadvantage." Of course, the actual "hands-on" experience with objects themselves will always make the strongest impression.

Another way of impressing the mind is through repetition. A principle may need to be repeated many times before it is heard. Do not hesitate to repeat lessons every so often. Many of the lessons are simply different ways of saying the same thing, and that is effective teaching.

At the end of each lesson there is a space labeled "Notes" which can serve as a great memory tickler. This is a place for you to record ideas before, during, or after the lesson. Record additions, alterations, examples, the response or questions of the children, and affirmation ideas. You may wish to jot down plans for augmenting the lesson, such as role playing, meditations, or art projects. It is always helpful to record how a lesson went over and suggestions for using it next time. Use this space to personalize the book and make it your own. The more notes you write, the more effective the book will be as a teaching tool.

Perhaps the greatest contribution these lessons can make will be to trigger similar ideas in your mind to better portray your philosophy. Hopefully, these activities will be a jumping-off place, and you'll start seeing in everyday objects a great many ways to expand children's understanding of this mental and spiritual universe.

GUIDELINES FOR AFFIRMATIONS

An affirmation concludes each lesson, so it is suggested that this section be read before beginning the lessons.

Affirmations, as used in this book, are positive statements about who we are, what we can become or experience.

What needs to be expanded are our beliefs about ourselves. We need to bring our self-awareness into harmony with the divine perfection that already exists within us.

All our beliefs are stored in the subconscious area of our minds. It is comprised of emotions, fears, doubts, actual happenings, and the accepted opinions of others. We cannot actually erase these beliefs, no matter how erroneous, because they've made permanent brain impressions. We can, however, cancel them by making stronger brain cell impressions which oppose them. This is where the tool of affirmation comes in. Because we are spirit, we are, in essence, perfect. We have a right to call forth that perfection by believing in it and speaking the word.

Of course, there are negative affirmations which we have unconsciously used all our lives, bringing about many unwanted conditions. We affirm negatively when we say, "I can't do this"; "I'm so tired"; "I think I'm getting sick"; "I'm such a slow reader"; "I am lousy at spelling"; or, "My memory is poor." Most of the time this kind of affirming, or self-negation, is carried on silently in our "self-talk," that steady stream of internal verbalization.

Anything we really want to change about ourselves can be changed by the use of positive declarations or affirmations. Words clothed with feeling have the power to impregnate the subconscious mind. It is a process of osmosis, as a stalk of celery turns red when left sitting in red-colored water or a white carnation is dyed blue when left in a dish of blue water. Other useful analogies are used in the lesson "The Power of Affirmations."

With young children, affirmations work very rapidly because children are closer to the truth about themselves. They have not had as many years of brainwashing to the contrary as have most adults.

Affirmations must be believable to the conscious mind before they will be fully accepted by the subconscious mind. The subconscious phase of mind is the formative power, and it will give form to what we feel is true for us now. It is the feelings that form, not the words alone.

Suggestions for forming affirmations:

1. Make the affirmation personal by using "I" or "My" or your name. Powerful affirmations begin with "I am." "I can" affirmations are also very effective. Use your name in the affirmation when possible. "I (name) am a good swimmer."

2. Word your affirmation as if you had already made the change you want to make—as if you were already the kind of person you want to be.

3. Use present tense, because future tense can destroy the value of an affirmation. The subconscious mind is very literal and, if your affirmation is worded to take place in the future, it will always be in the future. So avoid "I will...," "I am getting...," and similar statements.

4. The affirmation should indicate that the result has been achieved, not that you are "growing in it." Affirmations work best if accompanied by a visualization. It is easier to picture an accomplished fact than a vague process of growth.

5. The affirmation should describe the attitudes you wish to cultivate and not what you want to move away from. Instead of "I don't lose my temper," say, "I am even-tempered."

6. Do not compare yourself with others in your affirmation; such as, "I can write as well as Susan." Focus on you, "I express myself clearly."

7. Be specific as to the exact level you want to achieve. "I can swim three laps of the pool." "I play this week's piano lesson perfectly."

8. Inject feeling words into your affirmations to give them an emotional charge. For example, "I enjoy doing math," or, "I am proud of the fact that I am a good pianist."

Suggestions for the use of affirmations:

\# Affirmations impress the subconscious mind most powerfully when used in a very relaxed state, such as when falling asleep, when waking up, or in a meditative state. That is why negative thoughts held at such times can do so much damage.

\# It is extremely effective to have a mental picture accompany the affirmation. A strong picture can be worth 1,000 words. Our formative subconscious is very receptive to detailed visualization.

\# The more joyous the emotion one attaches to the affirmation, the more effective it will be. Feelings, both negative and positive, have formative powers.

\# Repetition is another key to successful affirming. Use it many times a day. Displaying it in several places can be a helpful reminder.

\# The more senses you involve, the more power you will add to the affirmation. Writing it, speaking it aloud, and even chanting or singing it are recommended for rapid results.

Further Suggestions:

The most important affirmations you can get children to use are those which build self-esteem. Self-esteem is the foundation of a happy, successful life. Many parents and teachers teach their small children to use the magic words "I like myself" many times a day. The friendliness and cooperation such words foster is amazing to those who don't understand that you can't like others unless you like yourself.

Older children can use "I feel warm and loving toward myself," or, "I love myself totally and completely." As already stated, their use is most effective when waking or falling asleep. They help counteract the bombardment of self-inflicted put-downs many experience throughout the day.

Training children to use an affirmation to greet their new day is always a good practice. "I am healthy, happy, and excited about this new day!" is one of many possible examples.

It is strongly suggested that the parent or teacher use affirmative prayer for the success of the day's object lesson. Write or say: The mind and heart of this child is open to receive the lesson at his or her level of understanding.

JUST ONE PERSON CAN LIGHTEN DARKNESS

Materials: Candle; matches; darkened room. Optional: candle for each child and paper skirt wax catcher to protect hands from hot wax.

Lesson:

In a home setting you might light just one candle and eat by candlelight while the lesson is discussed. Observe how little light it takes to dispel darkness. Talk about how we have a choice in this world. We can choose to be just like the candle and lighten the darkness around us. Ask participants where they think that darkness might be, since they don't frequent dark rooms. Suggest that most of the darkness they will run into will be in people's minds. It can take the forms of fear, self-pity, anger, sorrow, self-doubt, and thoughts of lack. The children might offer specific examples of these that they've heard or seen at school or elsewhere. Ask how they can help bring light to such darkness. They may come up with saying positive things to help the other person. Discuss the ideas you and the children develop.

Explain that at times it may not be appropriate to speak, but they can think loving thoughts about the unhappy person and picture him or her happy once again. Tell them that this picturing power is especially important when people are ill or injured. We can definitely aid them by visualizing them healthy, not as they appear to be. But we cannot decide what someone needs in order to be well or happy. We only send our loving, light-filled thoughts.

Suggest that in their prayers they might even visualize a bright, white light around the sad or ill person. This dispels darkness by creating a form of light that cannot be seen.

For additional discussion, point out how just one person with a candle can lead the way through darkness, enabling others to follow. Suggest that they can be the candle bearers and the candle they can carry is the Truth about themselves and all others. The Truth that each of us is a Son of God and made in the perfection of God can bring much light to dark minds. Offer some specific truths at their level of awareness.

Optional idea: Have each child light a small candle to show how much darkness is eliminated when several people are working together to bring light into a situation. Get suggestions as to where this light can be sent.

Suggested affirmation:

I enjoy bringing light to others.

Notes:

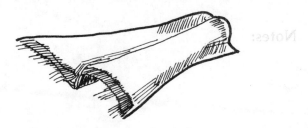

PRAYER MAKES THE DAY

Materials: A loosely woven piece of fabric about six inches square or larger. One edge should be hemmed, and the opposite edge fringed a bit. Optional idea: An unhemmed piece of cloth for each child, plus needle and thread.

Lesson:

This lesson is based on a quote from an unknown author: "A day hemmed with prayer is less likely to unravel."

You might begin by pointing out how the hem is preventing the edge of the cloth from unraveling. Pull a loose thread from the opposite end to show what can happen when there is no hem. You can even compare a fully hemmed piece of fabric with a completely unhemmed piece after each has gone through the washing machine.

The hem represents prayer, especially early morning prayer. The fabric is our day, and the unraveled edge of the fabric represents the troubles, irritants, and mistakes that can occur in one's day. The children can offer examples of a day that is full of "goofs."

4

Offer examples of prayers that can be used to start a day off on the right footing. This can include asking God to guide the day, affirming divine order for the day, affirming to be of help to others, affirming a state of peace and love no matter what occurs. With needle and thread each child might hem his or her piece of cloth as affirmative prayer thoughts are contributed or spoken in unison.

Here you can also discuss the powerful techniques of visualizing a happy day. Threads could be pulled at the bottom of the cloth to show what can happen if we pray amiss by picturing what we don't want.

Be sure to take some time to actually pray together and give thanks for God's guidance in all areas of life.

Suggested affirmation:

> *I start my day with prayer*
> *and let God lead the way.*

Notes:

SPIRIT IS EVERYWHERE PRESENT

Materials: Loaf of bread; pieces of various sizes and shapes torn off from it.

Lesson:

Give each youngster a piece of bread. Your dialogue might follow along these lines. "Do your pieces look the same? Even though they are different sizes and shapes, what is the same about them?" Help them to see that they are all identical in the ingredients that go to make up each chunk of bread. One doesn't have more salt, another more flour.

Explain that the pieces of bread are just like them. Each is made up of the same basic stuff even though their shapes and sizes are different. The loaf of bread represents Spirit or God and, since Spirit is everywhere present, it is in each of them. They all are a small part of Spirit and so have within them the God qualities of perfect peace, love, health, order, wisdom, and so forth.

7

Discuss how this is true of everybody in the world, no matter what they look like or act like. Each has the qualities of Spirit inside. Sometimes these are well hidden because the person doesn't know about them. We can help such people by looking for the love, peace, order, health, and goodness that we know is in them. There is no separation. We are all part of the One.

Suggested affirmation:

There is not a spot where God is not.

Notes:

TAKE TIME TO RELAX

Materials: One average-sized rubber band; a box or book that the rubber band will barely stretch around.

Lesson:

Pull the rubber band to show how much stretch there is in it, and then put it around the large box or book. Talk to the youngsters about what might happen if it were stretched out that much for very long. Tell them that, if a rubber band is kept under tension (stretched out all the time), it will deteriorate rapidly and break. We must allow it to return to its natural state (remove from box) in order for it to last a long time.

Discuss how people are very much like the rubber band. They also need to relax or they won't function as well as they are designed to. There's an old adage that says when things get tight, something's got to give. When people are under tension or strain, two areas that often give way are their health/or their relationships. The youngsters may have other examples, such as school work, piano practice, and so forth.

You may go on to explain that the best thing to "give" is some time for deep relaxation, because this will usually bring with it new attitudes or fresh insights. The best kind of relaxation for people is when they get very quiet and feel Spirit, their Source, within them. Some call this listening time or listening to the inner voice. Others call it meditation or getting centered.

Someone once said that real maturity is not growing up so much as growing in. Explain to the children that they have much inside them that is worth sharing with other people. If they take some time to relax and listen within each day, they can bring it out. This is the source of creative ideas if they wish to become more original. You might discuss what time of day would be best for them to get alone and relax with closed eyes for a few minutes.

Give each child a pretty colored rubber band as a reminder to take time to be quiet and listen each day.

This lesson could be especially valuable for overly active children. Also, it could be slanted toward a better understanding of the need for quiet time for the adults in their lives.

You may wish to take an extra few minutes and have the children do a relaxation exercise at this time. The simplest is to have them close their eyes, take three or four really deep breaths, and then think about a happy experience. Another simple but effective technique is to have them get in a very relaxed position, close their eyes, and hum on each out-breath. There are a number of books available now with centering or meditation exercises for children.

Suggested affirmation:

I take time each day to relax and listen within.

Notes:

LIKE ATTRACTS LIKE

Materials: A strong magnet or two; two bits of paper and pieces of tape; a tray of small objects, some containing iron or steel. Test beforehand to be sure the magnet will pick up a number of items. Know which ones these are. Most of the objects for the tray can be found quickly by a trip around the kitchen (e.g. paper cup, straw, toothpicks, pencil, paper clip, measuring spoon, potato peeler, jar lid, bottle opener, nail, spice can, scissors, egg timer, nut cracker, scouring pad, salt shaker, etc.). You may wish to let the children experiment first to see which items the magnet will attract. If they don't know it, point out the common denominator of these objects—iron.

Lesson:

Your dialogue could run like this:

"There is a law of mind that says 'like attracts like.' It's called the law of attraction or magnetism. Let me show you how it works. We'll pretend that these items are all thoughts, including this magnet. Let's say that this magnet is a happy thought. (Label it with a slip of paper.) It thinks, 'I have so many neat friends.' Now here are two objects; one is a happy thought, 'I'm a good singer,' (hold up a magnetic object), and the other is sad, 'I'm awful at sports.' (hold up a non-magnetic object). Which thought do you think this magnetic thought will attract? (Wait for response.) Remember the law is 'like attracts like.' Sure enough, it attracted the happy thought. Let's see if it happens again. This is the thought, 'Teacher likes me,' and the other is 'Sister doesn't have to do as much as I do.' Sure enough, it attracted the positive thought. Remove objects from the tray as they are used.

"Now let's take the other magnet (if there are two) or change the name of this one and label it an unhappy thought. Maybe it's, 'Poor me, nobody played with me at school today.' What kind of thoughts do you think it will attract? Remember the law. Can you name some unhappy thoughts? Each of those unhappy thoughts will attract another one (demonstrate with magnet and other objects). A person thinking happy thoughts will attract to himself happy, positive people that are fun to be around. If he keeps thinking unhappy thoughts, he will attract other negative people and ideas. That's the way the law of attraction works."

Suggested affirmation:

I am a happy person and attract only good to myself.

Notes:

THE POWER OF AFFIRMATIONS

Materials: Clear glass, ¾ full of water; bottle of blue (or any color) food coloring; spoon; bleach in small glass; eye dropper (straw can be used in lieu of eye dropper). For alternative analogy, have on hand a glass of small pebbles or beans.

Lesson:

(Best used after "Like Attracts Like" lesson)

Let the glass represent a person's mind, and the water the thoughts held in the mind. Point out how this mind right now is full of clear, clean thoughts. Elicit examples of the positive, happy kinds of thoughts that this water might represent. Have the children put in a drop of food coloring and call it a negative thought. Ask the children what it might be and have a suggestion yourself. (Examples: "I can't speak in front of other people"; "What dumb ideas I have.") You might say, "Oops! Here comes another negative thought," (as you add another drop of food coloring). What do you suppose attracted these thoughts? "I'm such a slowpoke." "Other people are much better at things than I am." Help the children remember the "like attracts like" law and that a negative thought will draw to it more negative thoughts.

Repeat the process of adding negativity until the water is a medium blue. Have the children think of prevalent negative statements heard at school or on TV.

Explain that the person with a mind that is full of negativity is probably feeling rather tired. It has been found that people burn physical energy three times faster when thinking negatively than when thinking positively.

Ask the children if they have any ideas about how one can get rid of all that negativity in the mind—all those fear, doubt, and limitation thoughts. If they don't know about affirmations, teach them about these positive statements that can work amazingly for them (see "Guidelines for Affirmations"). Explain that it often takes many of these positive thoughts to cancel out a negative thought. This is because the negative has usually been put in with so much more feeling or emotion.

Let the colored water represent one particular fear or limitation they may feel. Make up an affirmation to counteract it, and have them add a drop of bleach to the water. Have the children repeat the affirmation or similar ones while they add another drop of bleach each time. (Example: For a fear of being dumb or not as capable as others—"I am a smart person"; "I have lots of ability"; "I am a fast learner.") Stir the water now and then to mix in the bleach, and repeat until water is back to its clear, positive condition.

Alternative analogy to show power of affirmation: Use a full glass of water and enough small pebbles or dried beans to fill the glass. Compare the negativity stored in our minds to the water in the glass, and have the pebbles represent affirmations that can displace that negativity. Larger pebbles or beans can be used for affirmations put in (stated) with great emotion or feeling. Again, a particular limiting thought can be used, and the pebbles can represent specific affirmations. For instance, if the lack is friends, affirmations can be along the lines of: "New friends are continually coming into my life"; "I am a warm and loving person"; "I am responsive to other people's needs"; "I have friends by being one"; "There are an abundance of friends in my life."

Suggested affirmation:

> *I can choose how I want to feel*
> *by the way I think and talk.*

Notes:

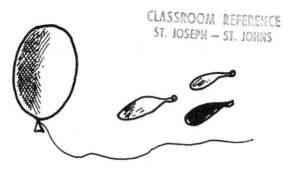

THE INSIDE GIVES FORM TO THE OUTSIDE

Materials: One balloon already blown up, and three or four extra balloons; could have balloon for each child (optional).

Lesson:

The balloons represent people—each one an individual person. State that each person is filled with the breath of life just like the balloons. Suggest that a child blow up a balloon by filling it with his or her breath of life. Help them to see that this same air or life is in all balloons and all people.

People only see the outside of the balloon or the outside of people, and they tend to think that's the important part. What's really important, however, is what is on the inside, because what's on the inside creates the outside. It's the inside that gives form to the balloon. Otherwise, it would be limp and useless like an uninflated balloon. (Show example)

We need to see the inside of others as more important than their outside form. Of course, the air inside us is important because it is what gives us life. Also important, inside us, are our thoughts and

19

attitudes. In many ways these help shape us and our experiences. But what is really important is the Christ within. You may prefer other terminology, such as Holy Spirit or God, for that point of perfection that all people share despite appearances.

Continue with the balloon analogy as follows: "Can you see that the life or air on the inside of the balloon is the important part?" Ask the child what happens to it when you release the air from the balloon. They'll see that the air rejoins the larger body of air outside it. You may then choose to compare this release of life/air to the death of the body. Help them see that there is no real death because the life force rejoins its source just like the air, and continues on in a different form. If there has been a recent death in the family, this could be a most helpful lesson.

Suggested affirmation:

What's inside forms what's outside.

Notes:

THERE IS NO SEPARATION

Materials: A silver or stainless steel teaspoon.

Lesson:

Compare the teaspoon to us, and the metal that was used to make the spoon to God (or Spirit).

You might explain it this way: "If we were to take all the silver (or steel) out of this spoon, there would no longer be a spoon. There is no way we can separate the silver from the spoon and still have the spoon.

"Now let's say that this spoon is like you and the silver in it is like God or Spirit. There is no way you can be separated from God because God is in you just like the silver is in the spoon. God is a special love energy that is in everybody and everything. Nothing is separate from God."

Explain, at the children's level of understanding, that the attributes of God are within them: love, peace, order, wisdom, understanding, etc. They can call upon these powers to activate them in their own lives. Even though these qualities are in them, they need to be affirmed or called forth. Use a particular example, depending upon the needs of the children.

For instance, if order is a need in their lives, they can know that they have this in them because it is an attribute of God, and God is in them. They can remind themselves of the order within by saying, "I am one with divine order."

You might suggest that they play a little mind game, and every time they see a teaspoon they think about God being in them just like the silver is in the spoon. Have them go on to silently affirm a God characteristic such as, "I am one with the love of God."

Suggested affirmation:

I am one with God.

Notes:

CHANGE IS NEEDED FOR GROWTH

(This lesson would be most useful when a child is at a place in life where some change is needed, where a risk needs to be taken. This could be something like joining Scouts or a soccer team, going away to camp, staying overnight with a friend for the first time, entering a new school, or whatever feels like a risk to that child.)

Materials: A tiny clay flower pot or the smallest sized cardboard transplanting pot; a tangled mass of string stuffed into the pot, and an artifical flower inserted into string mass. (A real houseplant that has gotten rootbound and needs transplanting would make the best illustration.)

Lesson:

Point out the mass of string, explaining that these represent the roots of the flower. Say that roots need a lot of soil to grow in, but these have grown so that there is hardly room for soil in the pot. At this point one needs to remove the plant from the old pot and put it in a larger one, or the plant will always be limited in size. Explain that people are just like that flower, and at times we, too, need more room to grow. Compare the pot to the children's old ways of thinking about themselves. The old pot, or ways, can be so comfortable that sometimes we need to push overselves out of this "comfort zone." If not, our growth would be stunted just like the growth of a plant is stunted when it's in a container too small for it.

The old pot met the needs of the plant at one time and was good for the plant. Now that the plant has grown, a change is necessary to enable the plant to continue its growth.

Discuss how, in order to grow and become all that they can be, they must change their old ideas about themselves. Help them see change as a means of "becoming." An acorn breaking apart to sprout the new tree, or an egg becoming a chicken, are excellent examples for this concept.

Suggest affirmation:

I welcome change in my life
because it helps me grow into greater happiness.

Notes:

OUR CONNECTION WITH GOD
AND EACH OTHER

Materials: Apple cutter. If this is not available, a picture or sketch of a bicycle wheel will do nicely. (An apple is not needed for the lesson.)

Lesson:

The wheel shape, as illustrated by the apple cutter, graphically shows our connection with each other and with God.

The hub of the wheel or center of the apple slicer represents God, or whatever term you use for the Almighty. We, the people, are the spokes. As can be seen, the closer we get to God awareness, the closer we get to each other. This works the other way around too, because as we get closer to each other we get closer to God.

When we're feeling really loving toward someone, we are kind, generous, and thoughtful. We are expressing God-like qualities. When we are angry and hateful toward another, we put ourselves further

27

away from an understanding of God. We can readily see (point to outside edge of cutter) that the farther away we are from another, the farther we are from God awareness.

Elicit examples of how people separate themselves from each other. You might wish to explain that that is why it is advised as the first step of prayer to forgive anybody whom you could possibly have bad feelings toward. Such feelings separate you from others and, therefore, from God-consciousness, which is total, unconditional love. It has been said that the only problem there is, is separation.

The more we work to express all the qualities that are God-like (peace, love, harmony, order), the closer we'll feel to other people. Other people will feel this and want to be closer to us. Together we move closer to complete God awareness. Encourage a discussion here of the ways that we can express God-like qualities in our everyday lives. Start with a personal and specific example.

Suggested affirmation:

The closer I grow to people,
the closer I feel to God.

Notes:

MY WORLD REFLECTS WHAT I PUT INTO IT

Materials: A small free-standing mirror; a hand or purse mirror for each child; a felt-tip pen; piece of dark paper and bright paper; teaspoon, paper clip.

Lesson:

Have the children play with the mirror and observe how it reflects whatever object it is pointed toward. Point out how accurately it pictures whatever is reflected into it. Explain that there is a spiritual law which works just the same way as the mirror and just as exactly. The mirror represents our world. The world picks up and reflects back to us our states of mind (our moods and thoughts). Another way of saying it is that we live in a world of mirrors, and all we see is us.

The mirror of our world is called effect, and our states of mind are called the **cause** of that effect. With felt-tip pen write EFFECT on your mirror. You might direct the mirror at a spoon, so that the child will see two spoons. Ask which is real, the one on the table or the one in the mirror. Explain that, just as the one in the mirror is only a reflection, all of life is simply a reflection of that which is placed in front of it.

If our minds are full of fear, doubt, or anger, the mirror of life will image that in our world. An angry person or fearful situation could come into our lives. If we're feeling sorry for ourselves, the mirror (life) will reflect back more experiences to help us feel even sorrier for ourselves.

At any time, we can withdraw an old thought image and place a new one in front of the mirror to bring us more happiness. Use a piece of black or gray paper to indicate a negative thought. Pull that away from the front of the mirror and substitute a new positive thought image (yellow, pink, or orange paper could be used.) Suggest some images.

Show what happens if you only half withdraw the unhappy thoughts and only half-way form new happy ones. Reflect in your mirror half black paper and half colored paper. Explain that one's experiences in life will be the same way—a combination of both the positive and the negative.

Another idea that can be illustrated with the mirror is that it can reflect large images just as easily as it does small images. Place a small item, such as a paper clip, in front of it, and then a larger item, such as a cup. Apply this as you see fit to areas where the children might be needing to think bigger and stop limiting themselves. The mirror, or our world, can reflect big dreams and goals as easily as small ones. If we don't think big, we can't expect big things to come to us. In all things encourage children to think their biggest thought, and then to think a little bigger.

Close the lesson by helping the children to see that we each need to put into our minds only the best, the kindest, and most unlimited thoughts because that is what will be reflected back to us. Affirmations can help us do this.

Suggested affirmations:

> *I look for the good in all things*
> *and the best in all people.*

Notes:

THINK ABOUT WHAT YOU WANT,
NOT WHAT YOU DON'T WANT

Materials: Two drinking glasses about 2/3 full of caked-on dirt; spoon; bowl; sink with running water.

Lesson:

Explain that we are the glass, and the dirt represents a negative condition or problem in our lives. We can clean out this problem in either of two ways.

One is by digging at it and scraping it out, which is what we do when we concentrate on the problem, trying to solve it. Scrape the dirt into a bowl, showing how the glass still isn't very clean.

Show that the other way is much easier because all you have to do is place the glass of dirt under a water faucet and let the water run on it for about five minutes. Do so.

The water represents prayer, a flow of positive thoughts and mental pictures that concentrate only on the desired result, giving no thought to the problem. The full attention is put on the end result, not on the means of getting it. The positive thoughts are best stated as affirmations. This method washes the problem away effortlessly, without struggle. If outer action is needed, we will receive that guidance in prayer.

While the glass is getting clean or clear of the problem, encourage specific examples on the part of the children. Name a problem familiar to them, and get affirmation and mental picture suggestions that can be used to wash it away. You may also wish to reverse the process. Display a clear glass of water (representing the children full of positive thoughts), and show how cloudy it can get with the introduction of even a small amount of negative thinking (dirt).

Suggested affirmation:

I keep my attention on the happy and good.

Notes:

YOU CAN'T GIVE LOVE UNLESS
YOU HAVE LOVE

Materials: Turkey baster; bowl of water; empty bowl.

Lesson:

The turkey baster represents the children and you. The water represents perfect love, which is unconditional acceptance and the absence of all negative emotions. In order to be filled with perfect love, we need to first empty ourselves of all feelings or emotions that keep us from accepting love. We cannot fully accept love when we feel unworthy or undeserving. Some of the emotions that make us feel undeserving are guilt, anger, jealousy, and resentment. These can fill us up and keep perfect love out of our awareness. Discuss such emotions and low self-esteem at the children's level of understanding. They know what makes them feel unworthy of an abundance of love. Explain that these are all up in the top of the baster, and have the child squeeze the bulb hard to eliminate this negativity. Holding it squeezed, guide the baster into the bowl of water (perfect love). Observe that, as the hand is released, love fills the baster up. Let the children experiment to see that, if the negativity hadn't been squeezed out, love (the water) wouldn't come in.

If the children are old enough, you can take the lesson the next step and teach that one can only love others as much as one loves oneself. It is love of self that can motivate us to clean out the bulb of negativity. The empty bowl represents "all others." With the baster full of love, have them share this with others by emptying the baster into the bowl. How much they have to share depends on how full they (baster) are with love.

Affirmations are a great way to replace negative thought patterns with positive ones and to build self-esteem. Help the children create some to suit their needs.

Suggested affirmation:

I am filled with love for myself and others.

Notes:

THE FORMATIVE POWER OF IMAGINATION

Materials: Scissors and paper for each child.

Lesson:

Point out that the paper represents the energy or substance of which the universe is made. The scissors represent our imagination.

Tell the children that they can use their imaginations (scissors) to cut anything they choose out of the universal substance. It has been said that imagination is the scissors of the mind. With those scissors (their imaginations) tell them they can choose whatever they would like to experience in life. Get them to think of specific examples and then cut symbolic shapes out of the paper. Initiate this by stating concrete examples of your own—a trip, a certain job or talent, a new home, and so on. Cut symbols of these from your own paper.

Explain that the imagination is one of the greatest powers we have and should be used with great care. Let them know that whatever they vividly imagine with faith on a repeated basis can come into their lives, so they must imagine only things they want to experience. Give examples of the use of the imagination as it relates to the children's world at this time (winning a prize, making a new friend, illness, failing a test, losing something, falling while skating, and so on). Remind them that they have the choice of using their imaginations either constructively or destructively. Also their imagination "muscles" need to be exercised like any other muscle or it may atrophy from lack of use. If time allows, you may wish to include some creative thinking exercises.

Conclude with a visual imagery exercise in which the children use their imaginations to construct some good they want in their lives. With their eyes closed, get them to image such things as:

— what a perfect day would be like from start to finish

— where they would most want to go if they could take a trip

— a school paper or report with an A grade on it

Suggested affirmation:

I use my imagination creatively and wisely.

Notes:

FAITH FORMS WHAT WE HAVE FAITH IN

Materials: Pre-heated oven; prepared cookie sheets and cookie dough for a cookie that will bake in about ten minutes. There are many such recipes available. If the lesson is done before school, do it early enough for the children to see the cookies come out of the oven and take some to school as a reminder of the lesson. If the second analogy is chosen, have a roll-out cookie dough and cookie cutters.

Lesson:

Let the children add the ingredients and help mix the dough if time allows. Discuss how each item is equivalent to thoughts, words, and feelings.

If time is not available for the above, at least let the children drop the cookie dough onto the cookie sheet, explaining that each spoonful is to represent one of their thoughts or words (verbalized thought).

Explain that the oven represents faith—that power which acts upon our words and thoughts. Say that "just as the oven has the power to take this cookie dough and turn it into yummy cookies, so faith takes your thoughts and words and turns them into experiences or things which we can see or touch." Faith actually draws from the invisible to the visible. For instance, faith that studying hard will bring an A on the spelling test or that getting chilled will cause a cold produces those results.

You may wish to use another analogy and let certain cookie cutters represent the "good" the children have faith in and expect to have happen in their lives. The cookie dough represents the energy or substance of which all things in the universe are made. Allow the children to experience shaping the dough into the "good" they want with appropriately labeled cutters.

NOTE: This lesson is best used after "The Formative Power of Imagination" lesson. Our imagination creates ideas of what we want, but it needs to be coupled with the power of faith to take shape in the physical world.

Suggested affirmation:

With faith in God, I achieve my heart's desire.

Notes:

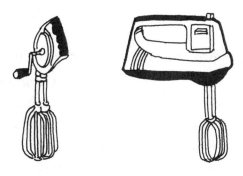

THE HARD WAY VERSUS THE EASY WAY

Materials: Hand eggbeater and an electric beater.

Lesson:

Demonstrate to the children how both of these tools do pretty much the same thing, but with one it's a lot harder work. Allow the children to try out both. You might whip up some soap flakes in water, or partially set gelatin dessert, or whipping cream. Lead them to see how much easier, with its various speeds, the electric beater is for whipping.

Explain that using the hand beater for a very long time can be exhausting. It is harder because it is detached from power; whereas, the electric beater is easy because it is attached to power. Point out the cord and outlet as the channel for the electrical power.

Discuss how the same is true with people. We have a choice of using the higher power, God power, or of not using it and going it alone. The latter way creates exhaustion and unsatisfactory results. When we ask for the help of the one power, we are tapping into the source of all love, widsom, and knowledge. We can receive guidance that is just right for our own particular project, and the energy to see it through.

If we know that there is a higher power, a spiritual power, which we can use, but we choose not to, it's just like knowing how to read and not reading. It's like having the instruction manual for a piece of equipment but trying to figure it out without reading the instructions. Would you rather make toast with a toaster or a candle?

Through prayer or meditation you can tune into the higher power, the one Mind. Simply ask for help or guidance and then quiet your mind and listen for what you are to do next.

Suggested affirmation:

I turn to a higher power.

Notes:

CHOOSE YOUR THOUGHTS

Materials: Put out several typical kitchen items from which a parent must make choices, such as:

2 packages or cans of soup
2 sizes of pans and rice package
a pudding box and a jello box
a grocery ad
2 or 3 similar recipes

Lesson:

Point out to the children that these items represent some of the constant choices you have to make in the kitchen: which recipe is best; which soup for dinner; which size pan for the package of rice; which is the best buy at the store, and so on. Demonstrate some right choices with these materials.

Share how we are continually making choices thoughout our day, though we may not be aware of them. We are constantly choosing thoughts and feelings. We're reaching out with loving thoughts or withdrawing because of fear. The one brings us joy, the other pain. All day long we have the opportunity to choose the thoughts that can either hurt or help us. When we're feeling anger, hurt, or other unhappy feelings, we can remind ourselves that it is really fear underneath.

The law of attraction says we attract that which we fear, so we want to be sure that we choose love thoughts, not fear thoughts. Love thoughts are healing and helpful, and they certainly bring more happiness into our lives.

If the children are old enough, teach that fear can arrive when there is a false belief in a power other than God. Since there is only one Power, God the good, there is nothing to fear.

Throughout the day we adults need to keep asking ourselves if we are coming from love or fear. Remember that more is caught than taught. We teach what we are.

Suggested affirmation:

I let go of fear and choose only loving thoughts.

Notes:

LISTENING FOR GUIDANCE

Materials: Large bowl of water; wooden spoon (or any large spoon); picture of something reflected in water (optional). Or, if possible, take the children to a lake or pond.

Lesson:

Begin by discussing how it is possible to look into a quiet pool and see the reflection of a tree that is growing on its bank. If the water is rough or churning we lose the image. Encourage the children to remember such a scene as you discuss the lesson.

Pretend that the bowl is the pool and the spoon (held vertically) is the tree. As you swish the water, explain that if the wind were blowing the water, or children were splashing in it, one would be unable to see the tree's reflection. Go on to explain, at the level of their understanding, that we each have a guidance factor within us. Some call it the Inner Knower, and others call it such names as Higher Self or Holy Spirit. It tries to speak to us and give us direction, but it can be heard only if our minds are calm and still, like a very quiet pool. The beauty of the tree is not seen in churning water, and the guidance of Spirit is not heard by a churning mind. An overly busy mind gives rise to problems. But when the mind is made very quiet, these problems are usually answered. A quiet mind can see beyond confusion to a solution.

Suggest they practice many times a day stilling their minds so as to be able to listen to the still small voice of Spirit. You may wish to suggest specific meditation techniques, such as holding a word in mind like "Peace" or "Love," staring at an object, or making a steady humming sound. There are many, many more.

As is possible with many of the lessons, role playing could enhance the teaching. One child could whisper a message, such as, "Call home right away," while another child is busy with noisy thoughts (churning the water) and not able to hear it.

Suggested affirmation:

I still my mind and listen within for guidance.

Notes:

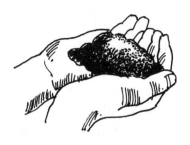

THINGS TAKE FROM ACCORDING
TO OUR THOUGHT

Materials: Baker's "clay" is suggested, but you may wish to use bread dough, cookie dough, play dough or natural clay. Give each child a chunk about the size of a small grapefruit.

Recipe; 4 c. flour
1 c. salt
1½ c. water

Mix ingredients and knead with hands for about five minutes. This inedible dough is popular for Christmas tree ornaments, jewelry and figurines. Objects can be dried at room temperature or baked on a cookie sheet in a 350 degree oven for about 60 minutes. They are done when light brown or a toothpick inserted in the thickest part comes out clean, showing that the dough has hardened.

Lesson:

Let the children play with the dough in their own way for a bit, and then suggest that it could symbolize the substance or energy of which all things are made. Since thought molds substance into form, suggest that they think of their hands as thoughts. You might even print thoughts on their hands with a water soluble felt marker. Have them squeeze, poke, and pull at the dough while thinking, "My thoughts are molding this substance." Tell them that this is how thoughts become things.

Next, have them form the dough into some actual things as a reminder of the lesson. Sometimes the things we would like to give form to are not easy to make with our hands, so we use symbols. "What could we make to symbolize happiness or love?" "What are some of the thoughts you want to mold into form?"

If they choose to make ornaments that are to be hung, a paper clip should be inserted in the top before drying or baking. Completed objects can be kept natural or decorated with felt-tip pens, enamel, water colors, food dye, or half tempera and half white glue.

Suggested affirmation:

I watch my thoughts because thoughts become things.

Notes:

THERE IS A GIFT IN EVERY PROBLEM

Materials: Several sheets of scratch paper and a pencil; a small wastebasket about ½ full of crumpled newspaper; a tiny gift box (with bow on it) under the newspaper. Inside the gift box have slips of paper with messages at the children's level of understanding. Here are suggestions:

— My problems help me to grow.
— Problems are friends because they help me become strong.
— There is a lesson in this challenge, and we are never presented with lessons until we are ready to learn from them.
— Within every disadvantage there is an advantage. I look for it now.
— Something good will come from this problem.
— My problems are learning opportunities.
— There are no bad experiences.
— What's the gift from this experience?

Lesson:

Ask the children to name some of the problems in their lives right now. As each is named, write it on a piece of scratch paper and invite the children to crumple it and toss it in the wastebasket. Older children may write down their own. problems. Suggest that they include anxieties about the future problems that may be of real concern. Have them do the same with some local, national, and international problems.

Explain that there is always a gift hidden within any problem or misfortune they may ever have, but they need to look for it. Hand the wastebasket to a child and ask him to look within the midst of those problems for the gift hidden there.

Have the child open the box and together read the slips of paper inside. Encourage discussion of these concepts, and be prepared with some examples from your own experience to illustrate them.

Suggest that in finding the gift in a problem it is helpful to rename the problem. Call problems "challenges" or "learning opportunities."

The children might like to have similar gift boxes in their rooms as reminders of the lesson.

Suggested affirmation:
(You may prefer one from the list at the beginning of this lesson.)

There is good for me in every situation.

Notes:

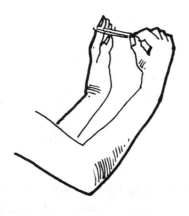

THE BOOMERANG LAW

Materials: A rubber band. Optional props that could enhance this lesson are: a boomerang, a yo-yo, a party horn that unrolls when blown and then rolls back up, or a Chinese yo-yo.

Lesson:

The Boomerang Law is another name for the Law of Cause and Effect — the basic universal law that is known by so many labels. The aim of this lesson is to remind us that we will reap what we sow.

Have the children observe while you put a rubber band around your finger, stretch it out and let it lightly snap back a few times. The Law of Cause and Effect says that what goes out, comes back—just like the rubber band. Whatever is put into the universe, in the way of thought, word, or action, travels back to the central point that sent it out. If one sends out friendly thoughts and actions, he or she will attract friendliness from others. Pull the rubber band to represent a friendly thought about someone. Now let it lightly snap back to represent good returning as a result of the friendly thought. Next have the children choose a critical thought, pull the rubber band out and let it snap back to indicate that criticism will return to them.

If you have a chinese yo-yo or a regular yo-yo, you can toss the yo-yo out and name a positive thought like love. As the yo-yo returns you can say love again, to represent love coming back. You may repeat this with a negative example as well.

"As ye sow, so shall ye reap" is another way of stating this universal law. If we are sharing and helpful, we'll find people eager to share with us and give a hand. If we hold fearful thoughts or act as if we are afraid of getting hurt or losing something, sure enough those kind of experiences will come into our world.

End on a positive note by emphasizing the children's fantastic, creative nature and their ability to choose what comes into their lives by choosing their thoughts and actions.

Suggested affirmation:

Only good goes from me; only good comes to me.

Notes:

THOUGHTS ARE GIFTS

Materials: Small box wrapped like a gift.

Lesson:

Begin by explaining that the little gift box doesn't really have a gift in it, but is a symbol of the many gifts we receive each day. Your dialogue might run something like this:

"For something to be a gift it does not have to be put in a box and have a ribbon around it. It does not have to be something that is bought. What are some of the gifts you like to receive that are not bought or wrapped?" Offer ideas such as a warm smile, a special favor, help when stuck or in a hurry, a hug or pat on the back, an invitation, a word of praise or appreciation, a promise to be taken somewhere special, a listening ear when we have a problem, prayers or loving thoughts sent our way.

"Do you see that you receive more gifts each day than you were aware of? How many do you think you receive each day? Well, I have a big surprise for you. In truth, you are receiving thousands and thousands of gifts each day. You do not consciously know about these gifts, but one part of your mind knows. How is this possible?"

You might continue the dialogue with: "There is only one Mind on which each person draws, and we're all part of that one Mind. That is why we say that all mankind are brothers. Because there is only one Mind and one Spirit, you are truly connected at some level with everyone on the planet. Each day thousands of people are giving gifts to each other, and these gifts are blessing everyone. The more thoughts and acts of joy and happiness in the world, the more joy you'll feel because of your connection with everyone else."

Elaborate on the unity of mankind at the child's level of awareness. If time allows, you may wish to include a meditation, visualizing all the world's people joyfully giving gifts of various types.

You may want to expand the lesson by stating that they in turn are giving gifts to brothers and sisters around the world when they befriend or help others or think loving thoughts. Each time they give any sort of gift they are blessing multitudes of others. The children could write "thought gifts" they would like to send out on slips of paper and place them in the box. These can be re-read or added to when they have a special need. As with many of the lessons, this lesson can be effectively offered via one or two puppets.

Suggested affirmation:

> *Today I rejoice because of the*
> *many gifts I give and receive.*

Notes:

THE ASPECTS OF MIND

Materials: Kitchen funnel. Put a strip of non-transparent tape around the funnel just above the stem, as shown in the diagram. As an alternative, heavy paper could be shaped to represent the cone of a funnel, and a paper tube insert could form the stem.

Lesson:

The aspects of mind discussed in this lesson are the conscious, the subconscious, and the super-conscious.

Lead the discussion along these lines, adapting to the youngsters' levels of understanding: "This funnel represents you and me. We'll call it a symbol. This small stem is our bodies. This large cone area represents our minds. The mind has two aspects or parts—the conscious mind, which you are well aware of, and the subconsious part, of which most people are unaware. These aspects of mind make up what we experience as our personalities.

"The narrow strip of tape next to the body or stem represents the conscious mind—the part of the mind you think with. It senses, reasons, evaluates, and chooses. Because it can make choices, it is known as the decision-maker. Because it has the power to make decisions, it is the ruler of our lives.

"The rest of our minds, the much larger portion, is the powerful subconscious. It is exciting to know about because it does so many wonderful things for us. It builds, repairs, and operates the body. It is in charge of all the body processes, such as heartbeat, blood circulation, digestion, and elimination. It is the storehouse of memory and the seat of emotion, habit, and instinct. There are some things it does not do. It cannot think, reason, judge, or reject like our conscious mind does. Since the subconscious cannot do these things, it is under the control of the conscious mind. It can be compared to a computer which is under the control of the computer programmer, the person who puts information into the computer." For younger children, consider the analogy of a gardener planting seeds in the soil, which is comparable to the subconscious mind. The soil accepts all seeds from the gardener, just as the subconscious accepts all suggestions or directions from the conscious mind. Now here's the good news: This phase of the mind has the ability to form. It can take any direction or belief our conscious minds give it and give it form.

(Note: Here would be a good place to offer some examples from your own experience. Think of times when you instructed the subconscious and, being the malleable substance it is, it formed according to your belief. Offer both negative and positive examples of having spoken your word or held a belief and seen it come into existence. You might want to suggest a simple experiment the children can test this on. A popular one is waking and getting up so many minutes earlier than usual without benefit of alarm. Have them set their mental alarm fifteen minutes earlier tomorrow morning by stating as they go to sleep that they will be wide awake and eager to hop out of bed at that time. If the children's understanding level allows, go on to explain about the superconsious Mind.)

Going back to the funnel, explain that the ability of the subconscious to form is unlimited because it opens up, as can be seen, to the great sea of mind we call the superconscious or universal Mind. This is the Mind that knows everything and can answer our questions if we get quiet and really listen. We always have the choice between letting the limited conscious mind direct our computer mind or inviting in the unlimited, all-knowing power of the superconscious. We do the latter by first asking and then quieting our conscious minds and listening within. It can guide us much more accurately than the limited thinking and reasoning ability of our conscious minds. This is why some people meditate or have a "listening time" every day.

There are many affirmations that can relate to this lesson enabling the children to take more control of the directing ability of the conscious mind and listen within to the superconscious.

Suggested affirmation:

I think only of good things that I want to happen.

(Remind them that the subconscious will accept their
habitual thoughts and give them form.)

Notes:

DO YOUR WORDS HAVE WEIGHTS OR WINGS?

Materials: Two pieces of paper or cardboard folded in half to make stand-up signs. Print "FEEL GOOD" on one sign and "FEEL BAD" on the other; pile of single words cut out of a newspaper or magazine. If children are participating not just observing, have about a dozen per child.

Lesson:

Our words may weigh others down or lift them up. They can help others to feel bad or to feel good. The same idea applies to our thoughts because words are just symbols of thoughts. Have the children place the words in front of them and form an arrow with them. Usually everything we say points toward either a good feeling or a bad feeling. They might shift their arrows in the direction of the appropriate sign as sample statements are offered.

The words that lead toward "FEEL BAD" are the words that weigh people down and make them feel heavy, discouraged, limited, lacking, or fearful in some way. This includes not just put-downs but the reporting of negative news, criticism, probing, or anything that creates the illusion of separation between people. All words that point toward "FEEL BAD" are a form of separation because they ignore that the other person is also a Holy Son of God.

Words that point toward "FEEL GOOD" are sincere words that lift people, lighten them, make them feel capable, lovable, and positive. Such words make people feel good about themselves, others, and about their world. "FEEL GOOD" words bring light into the mind and heart, while words pointing toward "FEEL BAD" bring darkness.

Suggest that they become careful observers of people's reactions so that they will know how other people are responding to their words.

The focus has been on the effect of words or thoughts on others. Make sure the children understand that their own words can also have a powerful effect on themselves. If they're thinking gloom and doom thoughts, being critical of themselves, speaking of lack or limitation, they are creating darkness instead of light in their minds.

This session might end with participants speaking to each other, using only words with wings, words that uplift.

Suggested affirmation:

> *My words have wings;*
> *they are uplifting.*

Notes:

MY THOUGHTS JOIN ALL OTHERS

Materials: Strainer; large bowl; spoon; package or dish of flour; cinnamon (or instant tea or coffee).

Lesson:

The bowl stands for the thought world—the thought atmosphere that surrounds us all; the strainer represents our minds, each person's individual mind; the flour and cinnamon are our thoughts.

Elicit a happy or loving thought from one of the youngsters and have him or her put a spoonful of flour representing that thought into the strainer. Give the strainer a shake (a child might enjoy doing this), and watch how these happy thoughts leave the individual mind and spread out into the world of thought—the one Mind. Explain how minds are joined in this thought atmosphere and because of this no one is alone in experiencing the effects of his thinking. Everyone feels a little happier because of that joyful thought that just went out.

You might go on to say, "Let's see what would happen if one of you put an unhappy or fearful thought into your mind." Invite a youngster to share such a thought while dropping a spoonful of cinnamon into the strainer. As the strainer is shaken or the thought is stirred around in mind, observe together how it permeates the thought atmosphere just as effectively as the happy thought. Get conclusions from the youngsters that some people might choose to be a bit more unhappy because of that thought.

If the children are old enough, discuss how, because minds are joined, we can tune into another's thoughts and they to ours. They may have examples of when they knew what someone was going to say or do before it was done, or of when others tuned into what they were thinking.

You could extend the conversation to "race consciousness" (concepts accepted by most or all of mankind that limit spiritual realization), and how this can affect us even thought we're not aware of it. Examples of collective or race thinking might be offered as spoonsful of flour or cinnamon go into the strainer. The TV, radio, and newspaper are often good sources of group thinking. Be sure to talk about how we can choose our experience. We do not need to be victims of the world's thinking, such as, "Now is the flu season."

Suggested affirmation:

My thoughts affect the entire world.

Notes:

ONLY OUR THOUGHTS HURT US

Materials: Pencils and small pieces of paper for each participant; three boxes about the same size. Small cereal, pudding, or gelatin boxes would work well for a small group of children. Tape a piece of paper with the word EXPERIENCE on the side of one box; a piece with the word UNHAPPINESS on another box, and HAPPINESS on the reverse side of the box. The middle box should have a piece of paper with the words A SECRET taped on one side and on the opposite side of the box tape the words OUR THOUGHTS.

Lesson:

Begin by having the participants think of an unhappy feeling they've experienced recently. This feeling could be anger, sadness, jealousy, resentment, or whatever comes to mind. If the youngsters are old enough to write, have them jot the word that best expresses their unhappy feeling on a piece of paper and put it in the box labeled UNHAPPINESS.

Next, have them write on another slip of paper the experience or condition that they think made them feel bad. Encourage concise statements such as "friend got invited and I didn't"; "fell off my bike"; "Dad wouldn't let me watch favorite program"; "lost my cat"; "Sister scribbled on my homework assignment." These slips go into the box labeled EXPERIENCE.

Now point out that between the two boxes there is a box titled A SECRET. This is a very important secret that few people know about. If the youngsters are aware enough, you can ask probing questions as to what must always intercede between an experience and unhappiness. Turn the box around to reveal the OUR THOUGHTS label and explain, in your own way, that the experience never creates the unhappiness. This comes from our thoughts about the experience. Another person can have the same experience and not feel the pain, anger, or sadness. Point out that they have a choice to "feel bad" or "feel good," depending on the thoughts they choose to think.

With the help of God they can learn to choose thoughts that bring happiness. Turn the third box to the word HAPPINESS. Share that the secret is that we can have whichever one we really want, the HAPPINESS or the UNHAPPINESS, by learning to choose OUR THOUGHTS. God can help us do that if we go quietly within and ask.

There may be volunteers who will share their painful experiences. Use these for group exploration as to how a different mode of thinking would lessen the pain. If no volunteers, have examples ready that are at their level of understanding. Focus on the positive options.

Just keep in mind that there is always someone somewhere who would not see that experience or condition as a reason to be unhappy. Our thinking creates our happiness.

Suggested affirmation:

> *I learn something from each experience*
> *as I turn to God.*

Notes:

WATCH YOUR WORDS

Materials: Bowl of water; salt shaker or small dish of salt; teaspoon.

Lesson:

This lesson shows that words once spoken cannot be taken back, at least not on the physical plane. We can reverse their effect, however, through prayer and positive action.

Tell the youngsters that the small dish or salt shaker represents us; the salt is our words; and the bowl of water is the other person. Shake the salt into the water and observe how the words have dissolved into the other person (if accepted). Personalize the demonstration by telling how you had an argument with someone once and called him names you were sorry about afterward. As you sprinkle salt over the water, explain, "These are the words I used—stupid, lazy, liar, crazy, loser. Afterward, I wanted to take these words back because I didn't really mean them. But do you think I could? Could you get some of those words or salt grains out of the water for me?"

Explain that both our words and thoughts go out into the ocean of thought around us and, just like the salt, can never be retrieved. Therefore, it is so important to think carefully about what we say. Before speaking we can ask ourselves if it would help the thought atmosphere or pollute it. Would it create joy or pain for the other person? Explain how the same is true of thoughts as well as words.

We can help neutralize negative thoughts by thinking "deny" and "affirm" and by substituting in our minds positive, constructive affirmations. We can withdraw a thought of someone as a "loser" by thinking of him as a "winner." Ask how we might lessen the saltiness (negativity) in our bowl of water? Will this work with the thought atmosphere? Positive declarations can dilute a lot of negativity.

Here is a good place to explain to children that all our mistakes can be corrected on the spiritual level by Holy Spirit. It is so important that children are not left with a sense of guilt. Teach that through prayer we can heal past errors and receive forgiveness.

Suggested affirmation:

I carefully monitor my words and thoughts.

Notes:

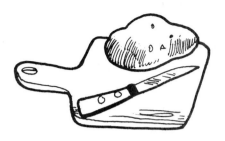

CUT YOUR PROBLEM IN HALF

Materials: Potato or lump or clay; small cutting board; knife.

Lesson:

It has been said that welcoming problems without resentment cuts the problem in half, and this is the focus of the lesson.

Life is God's schoolhouse, full of wonderful lessons to be learned from the problems we encounter. Our attitudes toward these problems are part of our lesson. Our attitudes can make learning fun or not fun.

Explain that the potato or chunk of clay represents a problem, any kind of problem the children might meet in life. Disclose that you know of a way to make that problem smaller, a way to cut it down to half its size. You might first ask for some ideas from the children. They may have great thoughts for making problems or challenges seem smaller. Share that one secret to cutting a problem in half is to cut or remove the resentment from it.

Demonstrate by cutting the vegetable in half. Label the removed part RESENTMENT, and show that that is what made the problem seem twice its size. When we let go of those feelings of annoyance, and bless the problem, not only will it seem smaller, but we will have freed up energy to use in looking for solutions. Resentment, like all negative emotions, is a form of fear and, consequently, drains energy.

Help the children see that when they learn to welcome their problems as interesting challenges, as opportunities for learning, as simply the lessons that life is giving them, all their problems will seem half the size.

Remind them that they never need to be alone in dealing with a problem or with resentment. God is always with us and can be asked for help. The spirit of God in us can turn resentment into love.

Note: This lesson has been successfully done with puppets. Use your imagination.

Suggested affirmation:

> *I welcome my problems as exciting challenges*
> *and turn resentful feelings over to God.*

Notes:

THOUGHTS DON'T LEAVE THEIR SOURCE

Materials: For each child, plus the adults, have a pencil, paper clip, carbon paper, and two sheets of typing paper. Place the carbon paper face down between the 2 sheets of typing paper, and paper clip them together. Before inserting the carbon, write in the corner of the top sheet the words "Other People," and "My Body and Brain" on the bottom sheet.

Lesson:

Have the children think of some happy and unhappy thoughts of the past several days. Encourage an awareness of both loving, kind thoughts and hateful, angry, resentful thoughts that they have had toward others. To aid the memory process, provide some real life examples of your own. With each one you recall, write the word on your paper. Have the children do the same, using symbols instead of words if writing doesn't come easily. For instance, a circle could stand for a love feeling, and a scribble for an angry feeling.

After the list is completed, look at the bottom sheet of paper where all the marks have been duplicated. Point out how all our thoughts and feelings left their mark on our bodies and brains. They didn't just leave us and go out to the other person. Explain, at each child's level, that the vibrations of the emotions affect our bodies and that thought makes an impression in our brains, which affects the way we see our world. Therefore, we can never give hurtful or hateful thoughts away. Whatever we're feeling is affecting us more than the other person. Sometimes the other person isn't even aware of our feelings. Whatever we give, the good and the bad, is given to ourselves.

One way to release the negative is through the use of denials and affirmations such as suggested at the end of this lesson. Also we can help ourselves by thinking happy, kind, loving thoughts because they have a healing and harmonizing effect on the body. You may wish to end the lesson by both children and adult putting on the paper some positive thoughts about specific people and then observing how these emotions were recorded on the body/brain sheet.

Suggested affirmation:

> (Denial) *I release all thoughts*
> *that are harmful to me and others.*
>
> (Affirmation) *I am careful to think*
> *thoughts that help me and others.*

Notes:

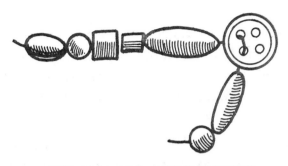

WE ARE ALL CONNECTED

Materials: A variety of beads or buttons (with two or four holes, not shanks); a long piece of cord or string. With a group of children you could have individual strings, or each could add beads to one very long string.

Lesson:

In this lesson the cord represents Spirit or God; the beads are our individuality or individualization of Spirit; and the colors, shapes, and textures represent our different personalities and appearances.

Have the children choose beads (or buttons) to place on the string and a name that each bead could represent—Dad, Uncle Charlie, Nana, baby sister, teacher, mailman, and so on. Put one on to represent each of them. Each bead or button should have a different feel and look about it, just as does each person.

Lead the children to see that all these people are connected by a common thread at the center of their being. This cord that connects us might be called

Spirit, or Life, or God. People have many names for it. Remind them that this cord of Spirit that connects us all is at the center of everyone. Make sure they know you are not talking about the center of the physical body.

It is good to look beyond the beads' various colors and shapes, or beyond people's different appearances and personalities, and to know that way inside, at the center of us, we are all the same. This center of us is perfect and is the most important part of us. If we just look at people as beads of different colors and shapes, we can feel very separate and different from others. But if we choose to remember that we are all connected by the cord of Spirit and Love, we can feel close to others. We can choose to look for this center of perfection within people rather than just looking at the outer person.

If appropriate, you might take a few minutes for them to still their minds and reach for that cord of peace and perfection, the Spirit within.

Suggested affirmation:

I look for the perfection in others.

Notes:

WE ARE A VISIBLE FORM OF SPIRIT

Materials: Bowl of cold water with ice cubes in it.

Lesson:

Explain that the ice cubes represent us (all people), and the water in the bowl represents Spirit, the invisible power of the universe. Through a certain process, water can take form—the form of ice. Spirit, which is invisible, can also take form and become visible. We are visible forms of Spirit, just as the ice cubes are a form of the water.

It is important to remember that the ice cubes originally came from the water, and not the water from the ice cubes. We came forth from the invisible to the visible. As when the ice melts and becomes water once again, at the time of so-called death, we simply lay aside our bodies and our spirits return to Spirit or the so-called invisible. To allay fears about being invisible or "nothing," explain that they'll be in a world which will be very happy and comfortable and visible to them. They'll simple be in spiritual bodies instead of physical bodies. You might explain that all is energy, but it changes form just as water can change form from liquid to steam or ice.

Suggested affirmation:

I am spirit.

Notes:

NOTES FROM THE AUTHOR

With a background of mother, parent/teacher educator, and student of metaphysics, it seemed only logical to bring these fields together in the hope of accelerating the consciousness growth the world is needing.

As a parent I felt a great need for more material on the mental and spiritual laws that was in a form easy to share with children. The result was the combining of three of my favorite teaching tools: Truth principles, visual aids, and analogies.

The saying that we teach what we need to learn never felt truer to me than when writing this book. I am joyous about sharing it with you who are rainbow climbers, that it might help you as it has helped me.

Since I'm already compiling ideas for Volume II, I welcome your comments on this book and any suggestions you want to make for the next volume.

A book of puppet skits using many of these object lessons will soon be available.

If you should wish a seminar, demonstration-lecture, or teacher training workshop, I am available.

It is my loving hope that you and the children on your Path have a glorious time ascending the Rainbow of Truth.

In love and light,

Peggy Jenkins

Peggy Jenkins, Ph.D.
3802 Park Knoll Drive
Port Angeles, WA 98362
U.S.A.